NICOTEXT

99 Movies
for people in a hurry

Text: Thomas Wengelewski
Illustrations: Henrik Lange

Copyright © NICOTEXT 2009 All rights reserved.
NICOTEXT part of Cladd media ltd.
www.nicotext.com
info@nicotext.com

Illustrations Copyright © Henrik Lange 2009 in agreement with Grand Agency.

Printed in Sweden, STC
ISBN: 978-91-85869-81-7

INDEX

8 The Karate Kid (1984)

10 Dirty Dancing (1987)

12 Star Wars (1977)

14 Ghost Busters (1984)

16 Back to the Future (1985)

18 Raiders of the Lost Ark (1981)

20 Gone With the Wind (1939)

22 Fatal Attraction (1987)

24 Casablanca (1942)

26 Radio Days (1987)

28 The Terminator (1984)

30 Alien (1979)

32 Blade Runner (1982)

34 Spartacus (1960)

36 The Third Man (1949)

38 Citizen Kane (1941)

40 Easy Rider (1969)

42 Taxi Driver (1976)

44 Some Like it Hot (1959)

46 Deliverance (1972)

48 The Bicycle Thief (1948)

50 Cinema Paradiso (1988)

52 The Seventh Seal (1957)

54 The Great Dictator (1940)

56 Lawrence of Arabia (1962)

58 The Shining (1980)

60 The Maltese Falcon (1941)

62 King Kong (1933)

64 The Good, the Bad, the Ugly (1966)

66 Jaws (1975)

68 Dawn of the Dead (2004)

70 Creature from the Black Lagoon (1954)

72 Showgirls (1995)

74 The Mummy (1932)

76 A Fish Called Wanda (1988)

78 The Breakfast Club (1985)

80 Mad Max (1979)

INDEX

82 Die Hard (1988)

84 Delicatessen (1991)

86 The Searchers (1956)

88 Psycho (1960)

90 The Battleship Potemkin (1925)

92 An Andalusian Dog (1929)

94 The Misfits (1961)

96 The Public Enemy (1931)

98 Rocky (1976)

100 The Blue Lagoon (1980)

102 Wild at Heart (1990)

104 Annie (1982)

106 The Sound of Music (1965)

108 The African Queen (1951)

110 Singin' in the Rain (1952)

112 2001 (1968)

114 Doctor Zhivago (1965)

116 A Clockwork Orange (1971)

118 Bullitt (1968)

120 The Sting (1973)

122 Rebel Without a Cause (1955)

124 Barbarella (1968)

126 The Evil Dead (1981)

128 Police Academy (1984)

130 The Blues Brothers (1980)

132 Yojimbo (1961)

134 The Bridge On the River Kwai (1957)

136 Mr. Hulot's Holiday (Tati): (1953)

138 The Guns of Navarone (1961)

140 Seven Samurai (1954)

142 The Thing (1982)

144 Escape from New York (1981)

INDEX

146 The Testament of Dr. Mabuse (1922)

148 Metropolis (1927)

150 Enter the Dragon (1973)

152 Jailhouse Rock (1957)

154 Cat on a Hot Tin Roof (1958)

156 Schindler's List (1993)

158 Brazil (1985)

160 The Wizard of Oz (1939)

162 Bagdad Café (1990)

164 The Big Blue (1988)

166 Scarface (1983)

168 The Godfather (1972)

170 A Streetcar Named Desire (1951)

172 Dr. Strangelove or: How I Stopped Worrying About the Bomb (1964)

174 Pulp Fiction (1994)

176 E.T.: The Extra-Terrestrial (1982)

178 Rosemary's Baby (1968)

180 The Exorcist (1973)

182 Breakfast at Tiffany's (1961)

184 Forrest Gump (1994)

186 The Shawshank Redemption (1994)

188 Goodfellas (1990)

190 Fight Club (1999)

192 North by Northwest (1959)

194 The Silence of the Lambs (1991)

196 Sunset Boulevard (1950)

198 Apocalypse Now (1979)

200 Platoon (1986)

202 It's a Wonderful Life (1946)

204 The Matrix (1999)

The Karate Kid (1984)

THE KARATE KID

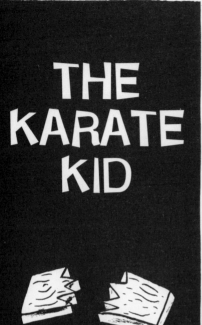

Daniel is a New Jersey teen that moves to California and pretty much deserves to get beat up.

He gets the kooky Mr. Miyagi to teach him karate so he can fight the bullies and get the girl. Miyagi just gets him to do his work.

Wax on wax off, MY ass

Daniel beats the mean Cobra Kai's with a ridiculous move that anyone could avoid. Mr. Miyagi should get arrested for child slave labor.

Dirty Dancing (1987)

DIRTY DANCING

In this coming of age tale Frances "Baby" Houseman is on a summer vacation with her rich parents in the Catskills.

She falls for dance instructor Johnny Castle and he teaches her to dance.

His big hair is attracted to her big nose and they end up dancing up a big storm. Boyfriends everywhere feel the pain that they can't dance like Patrick Swayze.

Star Wars (1977)

STAR WARS

A long time ago in a galaxy far, far away **Sith Lord Darth Vader** was having parenting issues so he does stuff like blow up planets.

Meanwhile, fatherless Luke Skywalker runs off with Obi-Wan Kenobi, Han Solo, and walking rug Chewbacca to find Princess Leia. They find a death star instead.

What does Luke do? He blows up the mechanical planet. Gee, I wonder who his daddy is???

Ghostbusters (1984)

GHOST-BUSTERS

What do out of work parapsychologists do to get a job? They start a sham about ghosts and pledge to save people from the specters.

What does a horny scientist do to get action? He convinces a hot girl that her apartment is possessed by the demi-god Zuul, a minion of Gozer. He doesn't get laid.

But they all get to fight Gozer on top a Central Park West high-rise. They save the city, blow up a marshmellow man, and Ray Parker Jr. gets a hit song.

Back to the Future (1985)

BACK TO THE FUTURE

Marty McFly has a problem - his parents are total losers.

Oh, and he gets sent back in time in crazy Doc Brown's DeLorean. There's that too.

Back in the day when his parents were kids he messes with their hooking up. Marty begins to disappear since his parents won't get together.

Marty gets his parents back together, invents rock 'n roll, and uses a bolt of lightening to get the flux capacitor to work for the time machine. Too bad he couldn't go to the future to stop the sequels.

1,21 Gigawatts!!

Raiders of the Lost Ark (1981)

RAIDERS OF THE LOST ARK

Indiana Jones is on a mission to make archeology look hip. He dodges boulders while collecting treasures and wears a cool hat.

And he has a thing for Marion who is basically a lush that lives in Nepal.

He gets in a race with the Nazis to find the Ark of the Covenant.

He wins, the Ark melts the bad guys, and gets lost in an American warehouse.

U-S-A! U-S-A!

Gone With the Wind (1939)

GONE WITH THE WIND

In pre-Civil War Georgia, Scarlet O'Hara defines high maintenance and wants to marry Ashley instead of Rhett.

Sir, you are no gentleman!

And you, miss, are no lady!

War breaks out and Scarlett has to leave her beloved plantation Tara. She still gives Rhett the cold shoulder.

When the war is over Scarlett marries Rhett and he eventually gets back at her and leaves.

Frankly my dear, I don't give a damn.

Fatal Attraction (1987)

FATAL
ATTRACTION

Dan meets Alex Forrest and has an affair with her.
The sex is good.

The follow-up encounters aren't so good and Alex cooks Dan's daughter's pet bunny.

Alex, just wanting some love, comes after Dan's wife with a butcher knife. Dan and his wife kill Alex and it saves their marriage. And it was cheaper than therapy.

Casablanca (1942)

CASABLANCA

Rick is the coolest cat in Casablanca. Everyone wants Rick. Rick wants no one.

But even Rick has weaknesses: mostly the beautiful Ilsa. Not to mention the smooth piano stylings of Sam. And Paris. Damn Paris!

Rick has to choose between the girl and helping the resistance. He doesn't choose the girl. Rick isn't French. Or smart.

Radio Days (1987)

RADIO DAYS

Woody Allen tells a tale about listening to the radio. People listening to the radio sound like fun. No?

Silly vignettes happen like the burglar who wins a prize for the house he is robbing by answering the telephone.

In the end the radio brings the family together with a false sense of security, until television tears it apart.

The Terminator (1984)

THE TERMINATOR

This is the tale of a poor little cyborg that goes back in time to save his machine friends.

To do this the cyborg Terminator has to kill Sara Connor, whose son will try to destroy the fun-loving machines.

But the Terminator doesn't kill her. He does get revenge on humans by becoming governor of California.

VOTE FOR

Alien (1979)

ALIEN

Alien-egg

In this yarn of unwelcomed guest, the spaceship Nostromos accidentally picks up an alien life form. Lt. Ripley is faced with the question: how do you get that unwanted person to leave?

You don't cut it since it bleeds acid. The alien likes to make a home inside people before breaking out and killing them too. It's bad guest. Didn't even bring wine to the spaceship.

Ripley, tired of playing hostess, leaves the party via an escape shuttle. But the alien, still wanting to party, comes along and Ripley has to push it out the door herself. It didn't even say thank you. Ungrateful visitor.

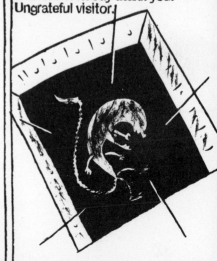

Blade Runner (1982)

BLADE RUNNER

R. Deckard is a blade runner in futuristic L.A where he chases replicants (fake humans). In L.A. Shocking.

Deckard chases and kills most of the replicants. And gets down with one of them, Rachael. It's L.A. - nothing unusual about having sex with fake humans.

Deckard finally sees the replicant leader, Roy, die while giving a great speech "I've seen things you people wouldn't believe…". But he's thinking about Rachael. Listening to fake people give speeches? Thinking about fake women? In Los Angeles? Is this really science fiction?

Spartacus (1960)

SPARTACUS

Spartacus is a pesky gladiator that leads a revolt in ancient Rome.

Crassus is a Roman general and tries to defeat Spartacus but just can't seem to do it.

Eventually Spartacus gets captured and crucified while his wife and child get to walk away.

The Third Man (1949)

THE
THIRD MAN

Holly Martins arrives in post-WWII Vienna looking for buddy Harry Lime. He finds out he was killed. Bummer.

He also finds out Lime has been selling bad penicillin for money. And that Lime is really alive and been traveling around through the sewers.

Martins helps the police get Lime. But Lime's girlfriend isn't happy about it and walks past him.

Citizen Kane (1941)

CITIZEN KANE

A reporter investigates Charles Foster Kane's dying word: Rosebud. Kane was rich but missing something.

"Rosebud"

Yep, the missing thing is happiness. But it really seems like having any material thing could make you happy. Who wouldn't be happy at the mansion Xanadu?

It turns out that Rosebud was Hearst's, I mean Kane's sled. Yeah, you have money for anything and you miss your sled. Sure.

Easy Rider (1969)

EASY
RIDER

What would you expect a film by Dennis Hopper to be about? Yep, Wyatt and Billy do a lot of drugs. And ride motorcycles across America.

They also sleep around and meet drunk lawyer George who gets killed in Louisiana. Wyatt and Billy go to Mardi Gras in New Orleans and do more drugs. Did I mention Hopper stars in   it too?

And what does such a life get you? Dead when your motorcycle blows up. At least you had the drugs and the wind in your hair.

At least for a little while.

Taxi Driver (1976)

TAXI DRIVER

Travis Bickle is a basic NYC cab driver: crazy, violent, and unbalanced.

He gets rejected by women, watches porn, and ends up becoming obsessed with saving a child prostitute. But, hey! It's New York.

With Mohawk cut hair he tries to kill a senator. But fails. He then kills a pimp and is hailed a hero. Anything goes in NYC.

Some Like It Hot (1959)

SOME LIKE IT HOT

Joe and Jerry witness a mob murder and run away disguised as female musicians.

One of the real musicians on the train is singer Sugar Kane and they fall for her. Hey, it's Marilyn Monroe-who wouldn't?

Joe gets Sugar and Jerry gets a proposal from millionaire Osgood even after he finds out Jerry's really a dude.

Deliverance (1972)

DELIVERANCE

When to fire your travel agent: when they convince you and your buddies to go on a fishing trip together.

And on the trip you happen to get violated by the local yokels in rural Georgia.

Squeal like a pig!

If that doesn't work for you then kill all the crazy hicks and go to Travelocity next time.

The Bicycle Thief (1948)

THE BICYCLE THIEF

Bicycle

+ Thief

= existential euro-flick.
Next time use a lock.

Cinema Paradiso (1988)

CINEMA PARADISO

Salvatore is a famous film director that finds out Alfredo, the movie projectionist from his hometown, has died.

He flashes back to when Alfredo inspired him as a child to do something great by teaching him to run a projector.

Yeah, that's the basis for launching a career.

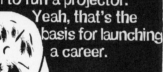

Alfredo leaves him a gift of a movie reel of kisses. Salvatore watches and cries probably realizing that Alfredo should have come out of the closet sooner.

The Seventh Seal (1957)

THE SEVENTH SEAL

In this slapstick, mad-capped, existential adventure Antonius Block comes back to Sweden from the Crusades to find death waiting for him. What does he do? He challenges Death to a chess match. Not my first choice but....

Hee-Haw! It gets sillier: A witch gets burned and Antonius asks her to summon Satan. Satan doesn't show and she burns. Hardee har har!

The chess match happens and Death wins saying "Nothing espcapes me. Nobody escapes me." Knee-slapping giggles all around.

The Great Dictator (1940)

THE GREAT DICTATOR

Charlie Chaplin portrays both a Jewish barber and Adenoid Hynkel, the dictator of Tomainia. Hint: Hynkel is Hitler.

Hynkel wants to take over Osterlich and convinces fellow dictator Benzino Napaloni to join. They get in a pie fight. See! Dictators have fun too!

The Jewish barber gets mistaken for Hynkel and declares democracy for Tomainia in a speech. This is where the Hitler comparison doesn't really work anymore.

Lawrence of Arabia (1962)

LAWRENCE
OF
ARABIA

T. E. Lawrence is a British soldier in Egypt during WWI that gets sent to recruit Arabs to fight the Turks.

Lawrence wins the Arabs over as he travels the desert, helping conquer towns like Aqaba. War is fun!

After being captured by the Turks he is raped and then war isn't so much fun anymore. He goes back to England and dies in a motorcycle accident.

The Shining (1980)

THE SHINING

"ALL WORK AND NO PLAY MAKES JACK A DULL BOY"

Q: When to consider a divorce? When your husband Jack books you to stay 4 months in an abandoned hotel so he can write his book? No. No divorce yet.

When Jack starts drinking with ghosts at the empty hotel bar and has an affair with a ghost in room 237? Nope, you can still work it out.

When Jack comes after you with an axe and tries to kill you and your son? Yeah, maybe time to get a divorce for irreconcilable differences at least.

The Maltese Falcon (1941)

THE MALTESE FALCON

"THE STUFF THAT DREAMS ARE MADE OF"

Sam Spade is the ultimate cool detective and gets hired by Brigid but realizes she is a crook too.

Everyone is looking for the kick-ass Maltese Falcon encrusted with priceless jewels. Spade gets it and has to hand it over to the Fat Man.

Fat Man realizes the Falcon is fake and leaves Spade. Spade turns everyone, including the dame, in to the police.

King Kong (1933)

KING KONG

Guys take note of this story: King Kong goes on a blind date and falls for Ann on his native island.

But he is tricked and taken back to NYC to be put on display as the 8th Wonder of the World. He still has the hots for Ann.

After the show he tries to keep the date going and takes Ann on top the Empire State Building thinking it worked for Tom Hanks in Sleepless in Seattle. He gets shot down by airplanes....and Ann. Beauty killed this beast.

The Good, the Bad and the Ugly (1966)

THE GOOD, THE BAD AND THE UGLY

Blondie, Tuco, and Angel Eyes are all after a hidden treasure buried in a cemetery.

Only Blondie knows what grave the treasure is buried in so the others can't kill him. But Blondie is Clint Eastwood so who's going to kill Clint???

In a huge standoff Blondie wins, Angel Eyes dies, and Tuco gets his share while Blondie rides off into the sunset.

Jaws (1975)

JAWS

What do you do when there is a shark nearby? Tell you what you don't do – you don't go swimming!

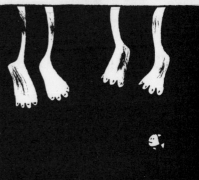

But people just don't listen. So with a hungry shark around – they swim! The shark loves it.

So how do you get rid of a shark? Get a drunken fisherman and blow the thing up. Problem solved.

Dawn of the Dead (2004)

DAWN OF THE DEAD

Question: What do you do when the world is being taken over by zombies?

Answer: You go shopping (at least that's what Stephen, Roger, Peter, and Francine do).

Until zombies take over the mall (probably starting at Sears). Then you fly away in your helicopter that has been just sitting around for some reason.

Creature from the Black Lagoon
(1954)

CREATURE FROM THE BLACK LAGOON

Poor Gill-Man: swimming in his lagoon when all these funny looking humans invade. He does the right thing: he kills some.

But there isn't a Mrs. Gill-Man so he takes a liking to Kay and drags her to his bachelor pad.

The crazy humans chase and shoot the Gill-Dude. Lesson: don't steal a guy's girlfriend even if you're a monster.

Showgirls (1995)

SHOWGIRLS

"I'M A DANCER"

It doesn't get much worse than this: Nomi goes to Las Vegas with dreams of being a showgirl. Big dreams start big movies.

Nomi wants to graduate from stripping to replacing show dancer Cristal. Cristal thinks Nomi is a whore. She ain't wrong. The names aren't the only thing that is bad in this film.

Nomi gets to be a famous dancer, her friend gets raped, she beats up the guy, kisses Cristal and leaves Las Vegas. Soft-core porn never got so much attention.

The Mummy (1932)

THE MUMMY

Imhotep is awakened from a nice nap of a few thousand years and isn't happy. He goes around in rags killing people.

What he really wants is his old lover Princess Ankh-es-en-amon who happens to be reincarnated as Helen and nearby. How convenient.

Before Imhotep can mummify Helen she recites a prayer to Isis and he dissolves. Sometimes prayer helps.

A Fish Called Wanda (1988)

A FISH CALLED WANDA

George, Ken, Otto, and Wanda steal some jewels but only George knows where they are hidden. He gets arrested and the others look for them.

Wanda goes after Archie, George's lawyer, while Ken fails to kill a witness but kills her dogs by mistake.

Wanda wins in the end by getting both the jewels and Archie and taking off. Otto gets rolled over by a steamroller.

The Breakfast Club (1985)

THE BREAKFAST CLUB

Q: What do you get when you put a jock, a nerd, a princess, a freak, and a trouble maker together at detention?

A: Neverending teen angst. Really, it doesn't end. But they smoke pot and dance.

In the end they are all still losers but at least they have each other. And detention to fall back on.

Mad Max (1979)

MAD MAX

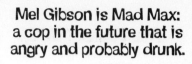

Mel Gibson is Mad Max: a cop in the future that is angry and probably drunk.

The highway gang led by Toecutter tries to kill Max's partner. This makes Max mad! (clever play on title, no?)

He hunts down and kills the gang proving that drinking and driving might work better in the Outback than in L.A.

Die Hard (1988)

DIE HARD

First mistake John McClane makes is to go to his estranged wife's work holiday party. You just don't do that. Luckily terrorists interrupt the party.

Second mistake is trusting the German since good ole Hans turns out to be the terrorist's leader. Up to John to save everyone.

Save he does in a standoff with Hans. He even saves his wife so he's out of the doghouse.

Delicatessen (1991)

DELICA-TESSEN

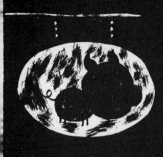

Louison gets a job in an apartment building in post-apocalyptic France. The currency is now food but these French are eating well due to the landlord butcher, Clapet.

Louison falls in love with Clapet's daughter Julie which is a smart move since Clapet kills and eats the people he hires.

Julie helps save Louison and her father dies.
They live happily ever after and the remaining tenants probably think hard about a vegetarian diet.

The Searchers (1956)

THE SEARCHERS

Ethan is an ex-Confederate soldier that hates everyone, especially Indians. Imagine how happy he is when Indians kill his brother and his sister-in-law and kidnap his nieces. Makes him ecstatic.

He spends the next 5 years searching for his niece Debbie.

Ethan finally finds Debbie who is now an Indian squaw. Ethan, being the romantic type, thinks about killing Debbie but ends up just killing all the Indians.

Psycho (1960)

PSYCHO

"A BOY'S BEST FRIEND IS HIS MOTHER"

What does a man with mommy issues do? He kills Mom and opens a hotel!

What does he do when a pretty girl comes to his hotel? He stabs her in the shower while dressed as his dead mum!

Eventually the party ends and he gets grounded in jail. Mom's not happy with this.

The Battleship Potemkin (1925)

THE BATTLESHIP POTEMKIN

Comrade sailors rebel against the tsarist regime after getting maggots in their food!

They take over the ship and sail to glorious Odessa where the proletariat welcome them and their fallen leader Vakulynchuk!

The tsar sends troops but they turn into comrades too! Long live the revolution... until it dies in an economic collapse 70 years later!

An Andalusian Dog (1929)

AN ANDA-LUSIAN DOG

What happens when two drunken surrealists make a movie? Eyeballs get sliced!

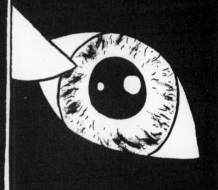

And a man gets to drag two pianos with dead donkeys, priests, and the 10 commandments on them to get sex. He doesn't get any.

It ends with the couple buried in sand. No, those surrealists never did drugs. No way.

The Misfits (1961)

THE MISFITS

"ANYTHING IS BETTER THAN WAGES"

Roslyn (Marilyn Monroe) is a gorgeous woman who meets cowboy Gay in Reno. Yeah, the cowboy's name is Gay.

Gay has the bright idea of selling wild horses to make into dog food. Roslyn does not love that concept. Conflict happens.

While Roslyn might save the horses, no one else gets saved. Most the actors in the film die shortly after as does Monroe/Miller's marriage. Good karma from this film.

Public Enemy (1931)

PUBLIC ENEMY

Tom Powers is a gangster that proves crime does pay: he is rich, has cars, and girls. Let's go rob a bank!

He even gets to do fun things like smash a grapefruit in his girlfriend's face. Crime rules! Let's go knock off a convenience store!

Well, maybe we jumped the gun: Tom gets shot and takes forever to die. So don't rob a bank! We're undecided on the convenience store though.

Rocky (1976)

ROCKY

Rocky Balboa is a lousy fighter that gets a shot at fighting Champion Apollo Creed.

Rocky gets ready for the fight with the help of trainer Mickey, hitting chunks of meat and running up stairs.

Rocky fights valiantly but loses and ends the film as a chunk of meat himself, screaming his girlfriend's name.

Adrian!!

The Blue Lagoon (1980)

THE BLUE LAGOON

Emmeline and Richard are young children marooned on a tropical island.

They grow up into smoking hot young adults spending the days fishing and swimming. They discover sex and life is great.

Then Emmeline gets preggers and, naturally, things get complicated. They think their son ate poison berries so they try to kill themselves by eating them too but are saved by a passing boat.

Wild at Heart (1990)

WILD AT HEART

Sailor gets picked up from jail by Lula and a snakeskin jacket, which leads to a 124-minute lesson that drugs while making a movie + Elvis don't mix.

Sailor robs a bank with Bobby Peru but it goes wrong and Bobby blows his own head off. Oops! Drugs + directing + Elvis are bad.

Sailor gets out of prison, again, and realizes he's a loser. But he sings Elvis to Lula as the credits roll. At this point the drugs are necessary.

Annie (1982)

ANNIE

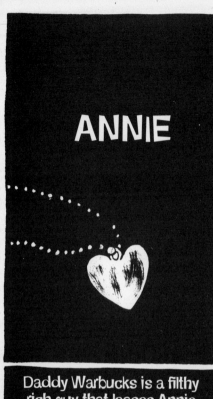

Annie is an orphan but also a player. She knows how to work a swindle. Orphans can't be trusted.

"The sun will come out tomorrow"

Daddy Warbucks is a filthy rich guy that leases Annie with no intention of buying.

Annie plays the "I'm going to find my real parents" card then agrees to an adoption/ merger and the dog comes as collateral.

The Sound of Music (1965)

THE SOUND OF MUSIC

Maria is a nun-wannabe who gets sent to be a governess for Capt. Baron von Trapp and his 7 kids. The kids hate her and her annoying singing makes them hate her more.

"Raindrops on roses and whiskers on kittens"

But she isn't as annoying as the Baron's fiancé Elsa so the kids put up with her constant attention-getting singing. The Baron, with a thing for nuns, decides to marry her.

The Nazis take over Austria and are so annoyed by Maria's singing they force them to walk out of the country.

"So long, farewell, auf wiedersehen goodbye and don't come back!"

The African Queen (1951)

THE AFRICAN QUEEN

After Germans take over East Africa and kill her brother, Rose Sayer takes off with Charlie aboard his river boat the African Queen.

Rose commits a major faux pas by tossing Charlie's gin but they still hook up along the river. Proof that beer goggles are overrated.

The Germans capture them and are about to kill Charlie and Rose right after they marry. But the German boat explodes and they get away!

Singin' in the Rain (1952)

SINGIN' IN THE RAIN

Dan Lockwood is an actor that can dance and sing and is not gay.

He dances in rain and never slips once and helps Kathy become a star. And he is totally straight. Absolutely.

Dan and Kathy fall in love and live happily ever after.... until the sequel: Singing in the Gay Pride Parade. Then the picture gets a little clearer.

2001 (1968)

2001

Discovery One spaceship is headed to Saturn with the computer HAL 9000 leading the way.

David Bowman decides to unplug HAL after the silly computer kills all the other astronauts. Bad HAL!

HAL

Bowman goes to Saturn where he's made immortal by going through a stargate that takes him to another universe. But he probably misses HAL.

Doctor Zhivago (1965)

DOCTOR ZHIVAGO

Yuri Zhivago is an orphan who is haunted by his dead mother's balalaika which he can't play but must carry around for 197 minutes.

Zhivago has a problem that most guys would kill for: Two beautiful women want him. Despite the Russian Revolution it is tough to feel sorry for him.

The war happens and people die and Zhivago gets Lara and kids are born and then he dies. The balalaika lives though.

A Clockwork Orange (1971)

A CLOCKWORK ORANGE

Alex and his droogs go around beating people and drinking milk.

He goes into rehab under the Ludovico method where he is forced to listen to Beethoven whilst being shown scenes of violence.

When he gets out, violence and Beethoven sicken him. So people beat him up. Being nice doesn't pay.

Bullitt (1968)

BULLITT

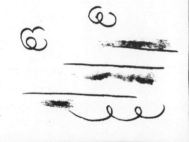

Frank Bullitt is in charge of protecting mob turncoat Ross before his testimony. But Ross gets killed.

Bullitt, being a bad-ass, chases the bad guys throughout San Francisco in his kick-ass Mustang.

He figures out the real Ross is still alive and gets him in an airport terminal. Bullitt always gets his man.

The Sting (1973)

THE STING

Henry Gondorff and Johnny Hooker are con-men out to get mobster Lonnegan. You can't trust these guys.

They bait Lonnegan with a fake off-track betting parlor.

Lonnegan losses $500K and fake feds scare him away. The sting works and Hooker leaves the money with Gondorff telling him:

"Nah, I'd only blow it"

Rebel Without a Cause (1955)

REBEL WITHOUT A CAUSE

Jim Stark is a high school rebel with a wuss for a father and monster for a mom.

He gets into trouble like playing chicken with stolen cars on a cliff. Brilliant kids here.

Jim's buddy, Plato, gets shot by police and Jim learns being a rebel doesn't always pay. He probably becomes a Trekkie. Less people die.

Barbarella (1968)

BARBARELLA

Jane Fonda is Barbarella: a space agent that has shag carpeting in her space-ship.

She is sent to find evil scientist Durand Durand before he destroys the world.

"The Reflex is an only child he's waiting in the park"

Durand Durand tries to kill Barbarella by the intense orgasm machine. Barbarella is woman enough for the machine and breaks it. Can you believe this was rated PG?

The Evil Dead (1981)

THE EVIL DEAD

In a shocking set-up for a horror film, 5 college students go to a Tennessee cabin for a weekend. Lesson: Tennessee is evil.

They find a book and tape (because people in the south can't read) of the dead in the cabin. Evil forces are unleashed. Some of the kids are turned into demons but what do you expect? It's Tennessee.

Ash, the lone survivor, burns the book and the demons go away. Except for one last demon that gets him. DON'T UNDERESTIMATE THE EVIL OF TENNESSEE!

Police Academy (1984)

POLICE ACADEMY

Steve Guttenburg gives hope to talentless actors everywhere as he gets work as Mahoney: a petty criminal that is forced to join the police force.

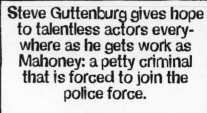

Mahoney tries to get kicked out of the academy but they want him to quit. Think of lowest common denominator for comedy and you'll be close.

Of course a riot breaks out and Mahoney and fellow ex-cadet Hightower save the day. They become officers. People probably lost jobs for making this movie. Or at least should've.

The Blues Brothers (1980)

THE BLUES BROTHERS

The dangers of religion: Jake and Elwood Blues are celebrating his release from prison when they get brainwashed by nuns and go on a crime spree to save an orphange.

They get in a car chase with cops through a shopping mall. All while trying to get the band together to help the nuns.

The band earns enough money but everyone is trying to get the Blues Brothers. They get thrown back in prison.

Yojimbo (1961)

YOJIMBO

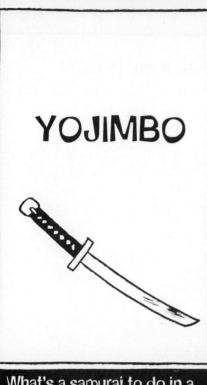

Sanjuro is a ronin in 19th century Japan that comes to a small town in a gang war. He agrees to work for both sides.

What's a samurai to do in a one-bit town? Use his sword to kick some small town ass! But one guy, Unosuke, has a gun. What can Sanjuro do?

He can cut him up like low-grade sushi. Which he does. And then walks away. Sanjuro's the shit!

The Bridge On the River Kwai (1957)

THE BRIDGE ON THE RIVER KWAI

In a Japanese prison camp, British Col. Nicholson goes on strike so officers won't work on building a bridge. Note that this was written by a Frenchman.

The strike works (written by a Frenchman) but Nicholson then becomes obsessed with building the bridge for the enemy.

A group is sent to blow it up but Nicholson tries to stop them. He's a little OCD. He later realizes his mistake and as he dies blows the bridge up.

Mr. Hulot's Holiday (Tati) (1953)

MR. HULOT'S HOLIDAY (TATI)

M. Hulot is a Frenchman on vacation who should never leave the house. He gets into funny mischief at the beach.

And wanders into a funeral. But holiday games go on and the slapstick continues.

But it is all life for the French in August.

The Guns of Navarone (1961)

THE GUNS OF NAVARONE

Their mission is to blow up German guns on the island of Navarone in WWII. Along the way they blow up a German patrol boat because blowing up German things is cool.

Captain Mallory is seduced by German spy Anna who is then killed by Maria. Lesson to Mallory: Think with the big head, not the little one.

They end by blowing the guns up and Colonel Starvos agrees not to kill Mallory. Starvos ends with the only girl left in the picture so that is why he is happy.

Seven Samurai (1954)

SEVEN SAMURAI

In 16th century Japan some farmers recruit 7 samurai to fight bandits.

The samurais fight the bad guys. The bandit leader shoots one samurai in the back. Not honorable but effective. He's later killed anyway.

So the farmers are happy they got rid of the bandits. The samurai realize they didn't win since most of them died and all they got was food. Time to unionize!

The Thing (1982)

THE THING

In the Antarctic an alien that can transform shapes is set loose by Norwegians scientists. Damn Norwegians!

The alien moves to the American camp. No one knows who is infected: who can you trust? No one!

So why not blow the whole place up? It's the Antarctic - global warming would've done it sooner or later anyway.

Escape from New York (1981)

ESCAPE FROM NEW YORK

Manhattan is turned into a huge jail and the President's plane crashes in it. Snake Plissken is chosen to go get him.

Snake lands in NYC and it isn't much different from reality: dirty, dangerous, and gritty. The Duke of New York has the President... and a sweet car with chandeliers.

Snake gets the Prez out of NYC even without a MetroCard and the world is saved.

The Testament of Dr. Mabuse (1922)

THE TESTAMENT OF DR. MABUSE

This little film is a testament to the written word. Dr. Mabuse is a loon that writes about committing crimes before he dies.

But psychiatrist Baum leads a group to commit the crimes. Lesson: don't trust a shrink.

The police capture Baum and, being bonkers, he pretends to be Mabuse and tears the testament apart. Leading to the advent of books on tape.

Metropolis (1927)

METROPOLIS

In the future Maria tells the working class not to revolt and that "The Mediator" will come to join the head to the hand.

Even though it sounds like it, it's not about masturbation

The ruler of Metropolis, Frederson gets a quacky scientist to make a robot to deal with the workers. It looks like Maria. Maybe this is about masturbation?

The robot incites a riot and the workers explode burning the hot robot. But Freder unites the rulers (head) and workers (hand). Make what you want out of the masturbation angle but people don't go blind.

Enter the Dragon (1973)

ENTER THE DRAGON

Bruce Lee is a kick-ass martial artist. He goes to a competition on an island run by the mysterious Han.

Lee fights in the competition and even kills the dirty Oharra. Han ain't happy.

But it doesn't matter who is unhappy because Bruce Lee will kick their butts. He kills Han, like that's a surprise.

Jailhouse Rock (1957)

JAILHOUSE ROCK

Elvis is Vince Everett: a no-good hoodlum intent on blasting that damned rock-n-roll. He gets sent to jail and starts a band.

Everett leaves jail and meets Peggy. They start a record label and Everett becomes a rock star. He should be playing Glenn Miller -it is more moral.

But he becomes a stuck-up jerk and it takes a fight with a jail buddy to teach him a lesson.

All because of that evil rock music.

Cat on a Hot Tin Roof (1958)

CAT ON A HOT TIN ROOF

Brick is pressured by his wife, Maggie the Cat, to make love to her while at Big Daddy's house. Bottom line is these people need names.

Brick has a secret passion for his dead friend Skipper. They were probably more than friends. Big Daddy has cancer.

No one has a real name. His brother is called Gooper. It's the South.

Brick has enough of mendacity and decides to pleasure Maggie the Cat. Big Daddy is going to die. Cartoon Channel gets lots of names for the next series.

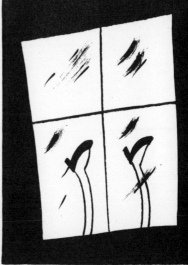

Schindler's List (1993)

SCHINDLER'S LIST

Oskar **Schindler** is a German that makes money using Jewish labor in WWII.

He makes loads of money and gets to be chummy with other Nazi's like concentration camp leader Amon Göth.

Schindler realizes it isn't all about money and saves as many Jews as possible making him a bad Nazi and a good human.

Brazil (1985)

BRAZIL

Sam is a worker bee in a totalitarian technology based society. He works in a government office but has dreams of a girl.

Sam meets Harry Tuttle, a renegade air conditioner repairman and terrorist. Sam gets associated with the terrorists.

The government tortures Sam but he dreams away and is happy.

The Wizard of Oz (1939)

THE WIZARD OF OZ

Dorothy is carried away in a tornado to a place called Oz and is greeted by munchkins. She makes an enemy with the Wicked Witch of the West and goes to find the Wizard.

Along the way she meets a lion, tin man, and scarecrow. There are even flying monkeys.

She defeats the Witch by pouring water on her. Then clicks her heels and goes back to Kansas.

Bagdad Café (1990)

BAGDAD CAFÉ

Jasmin, a German, invades and takes over a California café.

Bagdad Café has many strange characters like Hollywood set painter Rudi & tattoo artist Debby. Jasmin will cleanse them.

Jasmin accomplishes her program through blitzkrieg magic and cleaning. A new café and world order begin. The sequel has her invading Applebees for more living space.

The Big Blue (1988)

THE BIG BLUE

Jacques Mayol and his friend Enzo Molinari are professional free-divers that grew up competing against each other.

But Mayol has to choose between the ocean and love with American Johanna while going for the record dive in Sicily.

Dolphins or a hot American? Tough call. He ends up choosing the dolphins. Don't judge him until you have dated a dolphin.

Scarface (1983)

SCARFACE

"In this country, you gotta make the money first. Then when you get the money, you get the power. Then when you get the power, then you get the woman."

Tony Montana is a Cuban refugee that has a plan: use drugs and guns to get rich.

The system works and he kills and deals drugs and becomes filthy rich.

But Tony has a little addiction problem and a rage issue. Instead of self-help books he kills everyone he knows until he gets killed.

"Say hello to my little friend!"

The Godfather (1972)

THE GODFATHER

BUSINESS LESSONS WITH VITO CORLEONE:

Lesson 1:
kill your enemy's horse.

Lesson 2:
Kill the crooked police captain.

Lesson 3:
Kill all your enemies during your nephew's baptism.

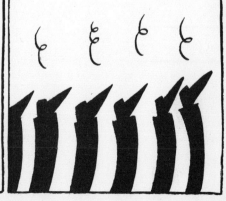

A Streetcar Named Desire (1951)

A STREET-CAR NAMED DESIRE

Blanche DuBois is the epitome of high-maintenance. She goes to stay with her sister Stella and her hubby Stanley in New Orleans.

Stanley is the king of his house and doesn't like having Blanche around.

So he does the logical thing to his sister-in-law: has her committed. Problem solved.

Dr. Strangelove or: How I Stopped Worrying About the Bomb (1964)

DR. STRANGELOVE OR: HOW I STOPPED WORRYING ABOUT THE BOMB

In order to cover up his sexual dysfunction, General Jack D. Ripper decides to nuke the U.S.S.R.

The President and kooky ex-Nazi Dr. Strangelove try to stop the attack only to find that the Soviets have a "Doomsday Device" that will blow up the world. Convenient.

The one plane that can't be stopped drops a bomb as Major "King" Kong rides it to the ground (remind you of another Texan with power?). The world blows up and that pretty much ends it right there.

Pulp Fiction (1994)

PULP FICTION

Vincent and Jules are gangstas working for Marsellus. Vincent is also a nifty dancer with Marsellus' wife.

Butch is a boxer who rescues Marsellus in a gang rape.

Jules decides he wants to give up the gangsta life but we never find out what the hell was in the briefcase.

E.T.: The Extra-Terrestrial (1982)

E.T.

An alien, E.T., gets left behind by his alien "friends". Probably because he talks in an annoying gravely voice.

Young boy Elliot finds E.T. and smothers him. E.T. wants to get out of there.

Phone home

E.T. finally convinces the other aliens to come back and get him the hell away from Elliot. In part 2 he gets a restraining order.

Rosemary's Baby (1968)

ROSEMARY'S BABY

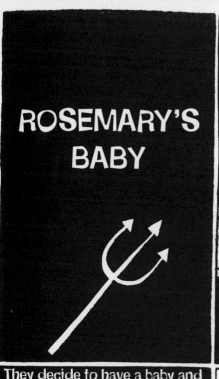

Let's talk about family planning: Rosemary lives with struggling actor husband Guy in the Bramford (i.e. Dakota) apartment building. How a struggling actor lives in the Dakota is a good question.

They decide to have a baby and after getting drugged up by the crazy neighbors, Rosemary gets knocked up. Guy's career takes off. Coincidence? Don't think so.

She discovers she was raped by the devil in exchange for Guy's success as an actor and gives birth to the bouncing baby Antichrist. Lesson: don't plan a family with an actor – it's evil.

The Exorcist (1973)

THE EXORCIST

Lesson in parenting: When your daughter starts speaking in foreign languages and stabbing herself, take her to a psychiatrist.

If that doesn't work and she starts levitating and claiming she's the Devil, call a priest.

If that doesn't work and she kills the priest then throw in the towel and sacrifice a goat to Satan. See where that takes ya.

Breakfast at Tiffany's (1961)

BREAKFAST AT TIFFANY'S

Paul's a writer and kept man. His sugar-momma puts him up in a NYC apartment where he meets neighbor Holly Golightly.

Holly is a gold digger that dates anyone with money. She likes to drool at the jewelry in Tiffany's.

In the end she falls in love with the writer Paul. Showing that even poor pathetic writers can get a girl.

Forrest Gump (1994)

FORREST GUMP

Forrest Gump is a slow-minded Alabama man who talks to strangers at bus stations. The kind of person you want to avoid. He also has a box of chocolates.

He seems to always brush with history, which proves that life is pretty much like a box of chocolates; you never know what you're gonna get.

And he somehow makes money and knocks up his childhood friend. His kid is smarter than he is.

The Shawshank Redemption (1994)

THE SHAWSHANK REDEMPTION

Andy Dufresne is a banker who gets wrongly accused of killing his wife and her lover and sent to Shawshank Prison.

Andy does the books for Warden Norton, which gets him benefits and prison becomes fun! He even plays the opera in prison before getting sent to solitary confinement.

Still, Andy digs his way out and escapes through the sewer. He steals the warden's money and goes to Mexico. So Andy really is a criminal. I guess crime does kind of pay.

Goodfellas (1990)

GOODFELLAS

This movie is proof that mobsters have fun and like to laugh. Henry and Tommy and Jimmy like to laugh.

"I mean funny like I'm a clown. I amuse you? I make you laugh, I'm here to fuckin' amuse you? What do you mean funny, funny how? How am I funny?"

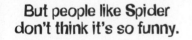

But people like Spider don't think it's so funny.

And, yeah, even Henry stopped laughing when the Feds busted him and made him talk. But it was fun while it lasted.

Fight Club (1999)

FIGHT CLUB

"First rule of Fight Club is: you do not talk about fight club."

Note: that stupid rule makes it kind of hard to talk about the movie.

North by Northwest (1959)

NORTH BY NORTHWEST

Roger Thornhill has some bad luck as he is mistaken for a spy and followed around the country.

He even gets chased down by a crop duster but avoids it. It helps that beautiful Eve is in on the plot.

He ends up on Mt. Rushmore where he saves Eve and the bad guys get killed.

The Silence of the Lambs (1991)

THE SILENCE OF THE LAMBS

Clarice is a FBI student who gets to meet good ole Hannibal Lecter: a fun-loving cannibal, to try to solve the Buffalo Bill murders.

Hannibal, in a lighthearted moment of buffoonery, escapes from jail by killing 2 policemen, and Clarice shoots and kills Buffalo Bill.

Lecter is still crazy but happy since he gets to eat his former psychiatrist. Everyone ends up happy, well, except the psychiatrist...

Sunset Boulevard (1950)

SUNSET BOULEVARD

Norma is a washed-up silent movie star wanting to make a comeback.

Joe is the lowest form of existence possible: a broke Hollywood writer.

Norma shoots Joe (Hollywood writer – not a big loss). As she gets arrested she gets on camera once again.

"All right, Mr. DeMille, I'm ready for my close-up."

Apocalypse Now (1979)

APOCALYPSE NOW

Yeah, Captain Willard has some issues: broken marriage, broken hand, and he has to exterminate Colonel Kurtz.

Willard travels to Kurtz up a river where he gets to know Vietnam personally.

He finally finds the Colonel who is insane and kills him.

Dennis Hopper

Platoon (1986)

PLATOON

Chris joins the army to fight in Vietnam. Seemed like a good idea until....

If the first casualty of war is the truth, then the second is a whole lot of Vietnamese civilians executed by Sgt. Barnes. Chris doesn't like it.

Chris gets revenge on Barnes courtesy of 3 bullets in the chest. He dared him to shoot, what else could Chris do?

It's a Wonderful Life (1946)

IT'S A WONDERFUL LIFE

Poor George Bailey wants to off himself for insurance money. Heaven mocks him by sending wacky angel Clarence.

Clarence lets George see life without him: Crime and loose morals abound with Mr. Potter in control. Basically a better place. George is being punished for naming a child Zuzu.

Acid trip over, George goes back to reality and people bail him out and Clarence gets his angel wings. Zuzu still has to live with the name though.

The Matrix (1999)

THE MATRIX

Keanu Reeves is Neo: "the One" to save humans in the future by defeating the machines. Yeah, Keanu will save society.

The Matrix is a fake reality created by machines to keep humans happy. Neo begins to master the Matrix and can do cool-ass stuff like dodge bullets.

Neo gets shot in the Matrix but is saved when Trinity kisses him and comes back stronger. Yeah, love saved Keanu, but not even love could save us from the sequels.